HOW TO BUY AN

EXCELLENT USED CAR

A Companion Guide For Women

HOW TO BUY AN

EXCELLENT USED CAR

A Companion Guide For Women

by

Leith C. MacArthur

1stBooks – rev. 01/11/01

What this guide IS:

A no-nonsense, no-frills, step-by-step guide that will assist you in the evaluation of the kind of car you already know you want. It is a 30 minute crash course in how to buy an excellent used car, cheat-sheets and all.

What this guide IS NOT:

This is NOT a guide to automobile insurance buying. This is NOT a guide to automobile pricing and/or negotiating the deal. This is NOT a 400 page technical treatise on how to service and repair your own vehicle. This is NOT a listing of which companies cars, foreign or domestic, may last longer than others, nor is it someone else's instructions on whether you should buy front wheel drive or rear wheel drive, sedan or wagon, convertible or roadster.

TABLE OF CONTENTS

1) An Introduction (or)

A Vehicular Nightmare...................................... *1*

2) The "Other" Woman (or)

So Now You Have To Buy a Used Car !....................... *9*

3) Hints, Tips, Tools, and What The Best Dressed Car

Buyer Should Wear *(or)*

Choosing A Good Used Car Is Like Choosing A

Good Mate. Now There's A Nice Little Bedtime Story.

.... *21*

4)Stormy Weather (or)

I Can See Clearly Now The Rain Has Gone *33*

5) Dandy Demonopolis (or)

Why Do You Suppose They Call Him "Sam The

Sham"?.. *37*

6) The Talking Car (or)

Are Your Ears Listening To What Your Stomach

Wants To Tell You? 47

7) A Little Help From Our Mechanics (or)

A Little Help from Our Friends 55

8) Go Get 'Em (or)

Go Get 'Em Twice 63

9) Crunch Time! (or)

Now Its Your Turn To Perform The Exam 67

10) The Obligatory Test Drive (or)

You Look Real Nice, But Can You Dance? 79

11) 48 Hours (or)

I Just Told You I Can't Wait Five Seconds! 87

Summary 93

Leith's Expert Score Card 95

ABOUT THE AUTHOR 99

Section 1

An Introduction

(or)

A Vehicular Nightmare

In 1991, Betty Kim traveled all the way from Deajon, Korea to Providence, Rhode Island. Her goal; to attend Johnson and Wales University. At 5' 4" and only 99 lbs. she was just 20 yrs. old and barely spoke English. Having little money and no American friends, it took great courage for her to make the journey, but Betty Kim held fast to the belief that in America, anything was possible. You are about to discover two things: that (A) Betty Kim was absolutely correct and (B) that this is not necessarily a good thing.

When I met Betty Kim, I was struck by her honesty and her openness, but I was particularly impressed by her vulnerability. She was one of the most genuinely innocent people I'd ever met and I wondered how she would get on in a city so strange, amidst a culture so foreign and so distant from her home and family. I knew that she would encounter many challenges and obstacles, and I feared as well that her sweetness and her vulnerability could very possibly bring her to grief.

One bright summer afternoon I received a phone call from Betty. She was in tears and I could barely understand her. After considerable reassurances from me, she calmed down enough to be able to explain that she had gone to an auto repair shop to obtain a new state inspection sticker for her car, a 1985 Pontiac Sunbird she'd bought for $1800. After having looked the car over, the manager of the shop (I'll not mention the name of the garage, but suffice to say it was a national chain that specializes in mufflers and brake work) told her that the car would not pass inspection, going so far as to suggest that her Sunbird was dangerous and should not be driven home. The repairs needed to make the car safe, as well as to pass the state inspection, would cost $900. (And, not surprisingly, he could do the repairs immediately.) Betty was despondent. She did not have the $900 and she would have to abandon her car. But then, how would she be able to juggle her tight schedule of school and work without her car? How could she finish school if she could not work? And if she could not work, how could she survive? She was in a near panic. I told her to take a deep breath, get the estimate for the repairs, and leave the shop immediately. I wanted to see that car. When she arrived fifteen minutes later my heart went out to her. Her face was streaked with tears and her fear was so tangible I could feel it reaching out to me.

When I read the estimate for the repairs I was shocked. Right there in the driveway I jacked up her little yellow Sunbird and crawled underneath, searching for the broken and worn parts indicated on the repair estimate. Not only could I find nothing wrong with the car, but many of the items listed on the estimate had *nothing to do with the state inspection that she'd gone there for in the first place.* After my cursory once-over, it seemed likely to me that the repair shop had fabricated the entire estimate. Betty and I immediately got in her car and went to a local garage that also offered state inspections. I was familiar with this shop's proprietor and knew him to be a fair and honest man. Saying nothing about the bogus repair estimate, I asked for a state inspection. After replacing a light bulb and one windshield wiper, our honest proprietor passed Betty Kim's car with flying colors. A sticker was placed on the windshield of the Sunbird and Betty was presented with a bill. The total was $23.75.

And the other guy wanted $900.00

So, you want to know the point to Betty Kim's vehicular nightmare? Its pathetically simple: the dishonest manager of the national repair shop "saw her coming," and this is what he saw: Betty was sweet, naïve, and vulnerable. Betty was alone. His conclusion?: Betty was not a woman, *she was a fish.*

Right then I realized that *who Betty was* presented a considerable, and sometimes frightening challenge for her in a world dominated by men. I decided on that day that I would do what I could to help educate her against the possibility of similar and future injustices. I would do the best I could to help her to change how she was perceived in certain situations. As it turned out, not only was this a good thing for me to do, but both of us benefited. She began to feel safer, and because of this I began to feel really good about being her guide. However, it would take a few years before I realized there was much more I could do. And it would take another woman to plant the seed of an idea in my mind before I truly got the "point" to Betty Kim's vehicular horror story and, most importantly, what I was

supposed to do about it.

Leith C. MacArthur

Section 2

The "Other" Woman

(or)

So Now You Have To By a Used Car !

Okay. So now you have to buy a used car. And, either by choice or by circumstance, you have to do it alone (or accompanied by someone else who knows nothing about cars either). Although you may possibly be a little excited, mostly you just want to get it over with. Most people DO just want to get it over with. I know. But please, listen carefully. Buying a used car without paying strict attention to the information outlined in this book would be like *pulling the pin on a hand grenade, sticking your fingers in your ears, and then praying that the thing won't go off.*

All right. I'll admit that's a bit dramatic. Buying a Bad Used Car (hereinafter referred to as a BUC, which rhymes with YUCK) may not be quite as dangerous as pulling the pin on a hand grenade in the middle of your living room, but it can definitely turn your otherwise bright dream of used car bliss into a dark and frightening nightmare.

Please use your imagination here: Its late Friday night and you're driving up country for the weekend to visit your old friend from college. Its dark. Its cold. Its raining. Its raining really hard. Suddenly, the car stops. Konks out. Just dies right there on the side of the road. You're ten miles from the nearest phone. You get out into the rain and raise the hood. You look underneath. (Everyone does this.) You stand in the rain for a minute, dripping, feeling the twitching bug of fear crawling in your stomach. But, you have a cell phone. You scramble back into the car, dig out the phone, and punch in the numbers for AAA. But the batteries in the phone are dead. This doesn't feel good at all. But suddenly, along come some headlights and now they're slowing down. Oh yes. You are about to be saved.

A big ole rusty cargo van pulls alongside. There are bumper stickers all over the faded paint. The stickers are hard to read but your mind vaguely registers a few of the phrases: something about "MegaDeath" and "Soft Tissue Damage." There are two guys inside the van, one with a long bushy beard. Each clutch a bottle of beer in a grimy paw. The bearded guy has a silver tooth. The other one has no teeth at all. No-Teeth leans out the window, grins, and says.. .. ..

Okay, so I'm being a bit dramatic again, but I'm doing it because I want to get your full attention here. Buying a used car is serious business, and it can have serious consequences, not the least of which can be the loss of your hard earned dollars. I know that you do not possess the expertise to go out and snatch up a trusty little used car with confidence. I know that it can be a bit intimidating, that you'd probably just as soon not do it at all. I know this because you're reading this book. And as surely as I know that you are reading this book right now, I know that if you continue to read it you will gain the confidence and learn the "tricks" necessary to guard against buying your own little vehicular nightmare. Its this simple; if you can answer questions like, "How many wheels does a car have?" or "What is the main function of the steering wheel?" then you're capable of conducting a transaction that will not only result in your ownership of a great used car at a fair market price, but will instill in you a feeling of confidence and pride, based in the realization that you have accomplished a formidable and foreign task with relative ease.

It really is easy.

Now, on to "the other woman".

A few years after I met Betty Kim, I had the great fortune to meet a woman named Joyce Reed. A dean at Brown University and the mother of four beautiful and intelligent kids who were all being put through various colleges by her (and as we all know, this requires a big giant pile of money) Joyce was in need of a good used car. Because of her obligations to her children, she knew she had to be frugal in her purchase. There was no room for error. I had an older, inexpensive Volvo wagon for sale, which is what brought us together. The instant we met, I could see in her eyes (just as the evil and corrupt manager of the muffler shop had "seen" into Betty Kim's eyes) that beyond knowing how many wheels a car was supposed to have, or what purpose the steering wheel serves, Joyce knew little of what it takes to avoid becoming a player in the universal game of used-car-Russian-roulette. Also -- and this is extremely important -- *she wanted help*. This made her vulnerable, and vulnerable is the last thing you want to be when you need to purchase a used car.

Joyce asked me point-blank if this Volvo was the right car for her. All I had to do was say "Yes" and she would have bought that car. (She admitted this later.) The truth was, however, that the car was *not* the right one for her. Although in average condition, the car had very high miles. In my opinion it needed to be cared for by a person who could climb underneath from time to time with a wrench and some muscle and some car savvy whenever the need might arise. No, I answered, the car was not for her. Joyce Reed sighed. The fear went out of her eyes. A trust had been established. Joyce then asked me to find the right car for her. I did eventually find another Volvo for her, and in the process I found a new friend. That was seven years ago. Since then Joyce has suggested to me on many different occasions that my ability as a writer (of novels), and my knowledge and experience as a professional car buyer, coupled with the fact that I have The Big I (integrity), makes me the perfect candidate to write the definitive book on how women (those women who know nothing of cars) can buy a good used car without, to put it bluntly, getting screwed.

Joyce was insistent about the guidebook. Throughout the next five years she'd ask, "When are you going to write that guidebook?" Finally I accepted the challenge. In doing so I had to ask myself two questions, A) Why am I so good at what I do? and B) Can I effectively convey in guidebook form just what it is that I am "so good at doing"? The answers are simple. I am good at what I do because I care about it, because I've been doing it for many years, and because it *is* actually rather simple. I rarely make mistakes when buying used cars because over the years, not only have I learned how to do something very well, but I've established some rules using this knowledge and-- here's the important part-- *I DO NOT EVER BREAK THESE RULES.* And, coincidentally, this contributes to my response for the second question, which is: Yes I can convey this to you in a guidebook format because all I have to do is *TEACH YOU THE RULES.* Then (it gets even simpler) all you have to do is *NOT BREAK THOSE RULES.* And here is the real beauty of it; you do not have to expend tremendous amounts of time and energy learning the mechanics of a vehicle in order to apply these rules. (Insert big sigh of relief.) Here's an analogy: If you did not know how to unlock the front door of a house, anyone could simply tell you to insert the key right side up into the slot of the lock and turn it. You would then know how to effectively unlock the house and get inside. You did not need to know how the tumblers in the lock worked during this process, nor how the key was cut, nor how the door was hung, nor anything other than the one right way to do it. This is what I will teach you in the ensuing pages. The right way to do it. The simple way to increase your chances of buying an excellent used car, and in doing so, *decrease* your chances of buying someone else's nightmare; a *BUC*.

Its almost as easy as turning a key.

In each section of this book I will teach you a rule. These are rules that anyone can learn and execute. Each rule is accompanied by points. At the back of this book you'll find *Leith's Expert Score Card*. When looking at a potential used car, you apply each rule, select the points earned, then enter the points on the card. When you're done, you total the points to determine the total score. Then you compare your score with my table. The score either PASSES or it FAILS. If it PASSES, you buy the respective car. If it FAILS, you do not buy that particular car. Even if you like that car a whole lot, even if it looks sexy and its your favorite color and you think you would just look perfect in it, YOU DO NOT BUY THAT CAR! After over thirty years of buying cars, I know that when I adhere to these same rules, I enjoy about a 98% success rate. Back in the "old days" before I got smart, I used to break the rules every so often. When I did break the rules (either because I was in a hurry, or because I got "emotional" about the car because I "liked" it) I would have only about a 60% success rate. Yikes. So, here's the biggest rule of all ----NEVER get emotional about a used car! I'm really trying to drive a point here. But if I'm not succeeding and you're just going to go out and buy the first used car you think you'd look good in, then throw this guidebook in the trash right now and go give up your fate (and your hard earned money) to Lady Luck.

Now, for those of you who believe in making their own good luck, let's learn some simple car-buying stuff.

Section 3

Hints, Tips, Tools, and What The Best Dressed Car Buyer Should Wear.

(or)

Choosing A Good Used Car Is Like Choosing A Good Mate.

Now There's A Nice Little Bedtime Story.

First , before you go shopping, here are some helpful little tips:

TIP # 1: *CHOOSING A GOOD USED CAR IS LIKE CHOOSING A GOOD MATE.* Okay, so now you really think I've lost my marbles. How can choosing a good used car be anything at all like choosing a good mate? (The operative word here is "good"). It's really quite simple. *IF* you were looking for a good mate, what would you be looking for as character traits? You'd want him to be capable of entering into a long-term relationship. (You wouldn't want him to give up the ghost and break down after just a couple of weeks, right?) You'd want him to be clean and in reasonably good shape. You'd want him to be honest. (Absolutely! He shouldn't be the type who's prone to telling those phony sounding **stories**. I know you know what I mean.) In essence, you'd want him to look good, smell good, feel good, be honest, have staying power, and most of all, you'd want him to be your friend. Well, I'm suggesting that you should expect no less from a good slightly used car than you would from a good used mate.

(Of course, there *are* a few things a good used car can*not* do for you—like paying for dinner.) If you wind up making an excellent selection in your search for a good used car, and this car treats you fairly, and you can always count on it, and it takes you many places and supports you faithfully throughout the years and the varied phases of your life, then this car *can* become like a good friend. I have, on occasion, witnessed tears at the parting of a few excellent relationships between car owner and good old worn out automobile. This is important stuff. Choosing a good used car wisely is an excellent thing to do. Choosing a good used mate wisely is an excellent thing to do. Simple, parallel logic. Only difference I see between the two is that it *is* *possible* to find a good used car. I'm smiling here.

TIP#2: *SERVICE RECORDS.* I'll not apply factor points for service records or for the lack thereof. On older, multiple-owner vehicles whose prices are modest, service records may not be available. However, please know that if you are looking at a newer car, say maybe $5000 and up, and your seller is either telling you that he's owned the car since new and treated it like a baby, or has treated it like a baby since he purchased it from its previous owner, yet he has no service records, he's probably lying. Period. Lying is bad. Buying a car from a person who is lying to you is stupid. Combine badness and stupidity, and you've got all the makings of your own little vehicular nightmare.

TIP#3: *INSPECTION STICKERS.* If the state inspection sticker on the windshield of your prospective used car is outdated, this is not good. If it is outdated by just a month or so, this probably means that the car would not pass the state's mandatory inspection and is therefore unsound or potentially dangerous and the owner is now trying to dump it on you (which translates into: It could cost you lots of money to fix it!). Accept no explanation but the truth, which should make sense. The truth is that the seller should have a statement (from the place that rejected the car during the inspection procedure) as to the repairs needed to make it safe and an estimate of their costs. If he has some **story** like -- Aliens kidnapped him and took him to another planet for the last two months and he just got back and is so traumatized that he can't drive and that's why the inspection sticker has expired and that's why he's selling the car – then you can pretty much conclude that he's doing what? That's right, he's lying. Now, if the inspection sticker is *way* outdated, like by two years, then this is not highly desirable either. You'll probably get a different kind of **story** for this particular situation which may go something like -- The owner either died or went insane and the car has been in probate or some other such nonsense. Don't buy it. Don't buy the **story** and don't buy the car. In my years of buying thousands of cars, I've come across maybe one seller who had a legitimate explanation as to why his car sat idle for two years; an explanation that was not as bizarre and unlikely as alien abductions or rampant familial mental illnesses.

Note: If you come across a car that's been sitting around for a few years, don't bother looking at it.

TIP # 4: *NO STORIES!* I'm sure by now you've noticed that I've emphasized the word **story** every time I've used it. My purpose here is to make the word **story** stand out. **Story, Story, Story**. There. During your evaluation of a seller's car, he should not be telling you **stories; stories** about why the car has a funny odor, **stories** about why the trunk is full of water, or **stories** about why the dashboard has several large bolts sticking out of it like Frankenstein's head. How's this for a nice little bedtime **story**? He just caught his ten year old son filling the trunk up with the garden hose so the kid could put his new pet frog in it, *that's* why there's water in there. No. Uh-uh. That is *not* how that trunk got filled with water. More likely that trunk got filled with water because sometime previous to your arrival upon the scene the car had been in an accident and now the hinges are out of alignment and the trunk doesn't seal properly and when it rains the water comes in and there's mildew in the carpet and soon the floor will begin to rust and then, and then, and then .. .. ..

So now you've got one of my most really very extremely important tips here! NO **STORIES!** None. Don't stand for 'em. Don't listen to 'em. Don't buy 'em. No.

Don't. Okay? Good.

MAJOR HINT, TIP, OR WHATEVER YOU WANT TO CALL IT # 5: Sometime before you go used car shopping, visit either a discount auto parts store or the automotive department of a K-Mart or Wal-Mart or the like and purchase a quart of 10 W 30 motor oil and a quart of automatic transmission fluid. Take them home. In your kitchen (or wherever there is good light -- maybe outside on the patio) open them.

a) First, pour a little motor oil on your index finger. Rub it twixt finger and thumb. (Twixt: I've been just dyin' for the opportunity to use that word). Notice how slick and smooth it feels. Ideally, you should remove the dipstick from your current vehicle, wipe it off, and pour the fresh oil onto it. Hold it (either your finger or your dipstick) up to the light. See how clean it looks, and how its devoid of particles? Note that it is nearly clear and devoid of color. Smell it. (Remember how it smells.) When you check out your used car and you pull its dipstick, the oil should be similar to this: clear, devoid of particles, and not smelling "burnt".

b) Now, do the same with the transmission fluid. Note how it looks and feels. It should have a raspberry tint to it. Note its consistency. *Smell it.* (This is big. Any transmission fluid that smells otherwise than the new fluid is indicative of a serious problem. You're more likely to notice particles that feel like sand and to get a parched or burned smell with transmission fluid than with engine oil. If you find particles in the transmission fluid, this is *very* bad.)

c) Keep your test fluids handy. The day you go to check out your first vehicle, just before you leave your home, do the "see-feel-smell test" once again to refresh your memory.

Okay, now on to the tools.

TOOLS: [Don't go used car shopping without them.]

Tool #1: A small flashlight

Tool #2: A small towel or a rag.

Tool #3: A screwdriver (or any pokey thingy).

Tool #4: Leith's "Expert" Score Card.

BEST DRESSED: However simple this may seem, it deserves mention. Wear jeans or loose fitting pants and an old gardening shirt or sweatshirt. You will have to bend down and look underneath the car at least once. Be prepared to get a little dirty (and of course, be prepared for the bending down part). So, you have your tools and you are dressed appropriately. Now let's go evaluate a car.

Leith C. MacArthur

Section 4

Stormy Weather

(or)

I Can See Clearly Now The Rain Has Gone

Okay. You've decided on the type of car you want and you've also decided how much money you're prepared to spend on it. (You should have some knowledge of what the fair market value is for your dream car. There are quite a few sources for this information. Try the N.A.D.A Official Used Car Guide, 8400 Westpark Dr., McLean, VA, 22102, 1-800-544-6232, www.nada.com, or The Kelly Blue Book, www.kbb.com. In my opinion, they both suggest retail prices that are a little high, maybe around 15% to 20%.) After perusing the classifieds you've made a few calls and now you have an appointment to see a car this afternoon. [During this call you must confirm that the seller will allow you to take the vehicle to a qualified mechanic to check it out for you. If the seller will not allow this, forget this vehicle and go on to the next.] You're dressed for the occasion, you have your tools ready, you notice that its raining. You check the forecast. Its going to rain all afternoon and into the night, but a bright and sunny day is expected for tomorrow. What do you do next? [Here comes a rule.] **You get on the phone and you change your appointment to another day.** Never go to look at your potential used car in the rain. Let me tell you why. First of all, the rain makes all paint surfaces look nice and shiny, no matter how dull or faded they may actually be, and sometimes the rain can even cover up a fender that's a different shade of red from the rest of the car because it was badly repaired after your seller had run the thing into a fire hydrant. Here's another reason for staying home when its wet outside. A car that's been driven in the rain will be soaking wet underneath, with droplets of water dripping off the engine and transmission and whatever else. Its virtually impossible to tell if the car is leaking coolant or transmission fluid or power steering fluid or engine oil when there's water dripping off everything. There are other reasons for not evaluating a car in the rain, such as your inability to conduct a simulated panic stop in an empty parking lot. (Its tough to evaluate the automobile's braking capabilities when your skidding all over the place.) Always check your car out on a nice dry day. The only advantage you might have by checking a car out in inclement weather might be that you could see if the sunroof leaks when it rains. But a garden hose directed onto the sunroof can tell you the same thing on a dry day, and the negative consequences of rain far outweigh its few positive possibilities.

When its raining, and you're looking to purchase a great used car that will serve you faithfully for the next five years, stay home and keep nice and warm and dry like your mother always said you should. Have a cup of tea or a nice bowl of soup. Wait for the sunshine to come. Buying a great used car requires focus, and you need all the elements of the universe working with you, not against.

LEITH'S EXPERT SCORE CARD:

You waited for the sun to shine:					0 points

You evaluated the car in the rain anyway:			**- 10 points**

Section 5

Dandy Demonopolis

(or)

Why Do You Suppose They Call Him "Sam The Sham"?

When I was in my mid-twenties I got a job selling cars at a very successful new-car dealership in my home town. It was my first real "sales" job. I'd been an auto mechanic since I'd gotten out of high school, and although I was very good at twisting wrenches, I wanted to better myself. Excited at the prospects of a new venture, I felt that my integrity and my years of experience with the mechanical aspects of automobiles would make for an invaluable combination in my new job. On my first day, I shared this belief with my sales manager. His reply stunned me. "You can forget all that honesty and mechanical experience crap," he said. "Just watch closely, and do whatever *he* does." With this the sales manager crooked a nicotine-stained finger at a man standing by the front door of the showroom. This man cut an imposing figure. Black eyes glued to the parking lot entrance, he wore a three piece, pinstriped, black polyester suit that glinted in the sunlight, and black, wing-tipped shoes so gleamingly polished you could see the fine points of his precisely trimmed black goatee reflected in their surfaces. A gold tie tack, a gold pocket watch chain that drooped across his vest, and three or four rings that looked like fat dollops of yellow gold on his chubby fingers all gave him an air of mercantile grandeur. Jet black hair greased and pulled back straight behind his ears back made him look so swift and fast, he appeared positively aerodynamic. Actually, to me he looked like the lead singer of the fifties group "Sam The Sham and the Pharoah's". This man was Dandy Demonopolis (absurdly fake name), the dealership's Numero Uno, their hotshot salesman of the year. He consistently outsold every other salesman by twice their unit numbers. But my lingering question was; Who would buy a car from this man, really? I mean, *Really!*

Many people, apparently.

I did watch him carefully, not because I wanted to emulate him, but because I just could not understand how he could sell so many cars. To me, he seemed the epitome of the slick and pushy guy who has become one of the most dreaded of all sales types, the "used car salesman". If I was smart enough to *know not to* buy from his "type", why then did so many others do just the opposite? I soon learned that most of his customers seemed to have something in common; they didn't know much about cars, and they wanted to have their questions and their concerns addressed. Demonopolis did exactly that. He gave them answers, regardless of how close to the truth those answers were.

He was the consummate pro. He was clearly a professional and he knew his product well. He was thorough and he would follow up on all his prospects. He was really pushy and he didn't let many prospects off the hook. He was all the things that most people say they don't want to have to deal with when trying to buy something. But this is what made the difference; *he told people what they wanted to hear.* He did one thing better than any of the other sales people in the dealership; he made out like he was friends with his customers and he seemed to give them what they wanted. He exuded a charm and warmth that was comforting to the point that upon meeting him one would soon overlook the slick persona. Everyone who is in the process of buying a car wants to be reassured that their choices are good ones. Demonopolis did just that for them. I saw him sell hundreds of new cars this way, and because they were *new* cars, none of his customers were the worse for it. But I saw him, on occasion, sell *used cars* off the lot in the same way, some of which may not have been very good automobiles. He told them what they wanted hear, he just failed to tell them what they *needed* to hear.

Why am I telling you about old Dandy D? Because I suggest that you pay close attention to the person who is trying to sell you their car. It is my opinion that you stand a better chance of buying a good used car from a private party than you do from a used car lot. I'm simply talking odds here. I know there are many reputable and honest used car salesman out there. Its not my intention to denigrate them. But, unfortunately there are a whole gaggle of used car salesman who are more interested in cash than they are in the veracity of their claims. The term "used car salesman" did not become the universal symbol of distrust for no reason at all.

That said, many prefer to go to used car lots and shop as one might in a department store rather than to seek out individual private owners. They feel they can see more cars, and they are right. If you are one who feels this way, and you wish to go to the used car lots also, you have my blessing. Just be very careful and use your God-given woman's intuition. If the feeling in the pit of our stomach is telling you that the salesman you're dealing with (or the private owner, for that matter) is lying to you, then you are increasing the odds that you will purchase a vehicle that is something other than what was presented to you. You don't want to be the one to buy a car that had been submerged in flood waters somewhere in the mid-west, then cleaned and doctored up and shipped into your state and palmed off as a recent trade-in from some fictitious little old lady who took oh so meticulous care of her car. (This did happen with hundreds of cars that were drowned in the disastrous floods a few years ago, and it continues to happen to this day. Its common practice for new and used car dealers alike to send their pro buyers into other parts of the country seeking to purchase bulk amounts of vehicles at wholesale, which would then be then shipped to their dealerships and sold on their lots.) Pay as close attention to your seller as you do to his or her car. Follow your gut instincts. If you don't like the seller, but you ignore this and go ahead and buy the car because it looks like what you want, then there is a good chance that eventually you'll find that you don't like the car either.

Leith's "Demonopolis Rule": ***Never expect more from a car than you'd expect from its owner.***

LEITH'S EXPERT SCORE CARD

You like and trust the seller: 0 points

You dislike or distrust the seller,

you just don't feel comfortable: **- 5 points**

Leith C. MacArthur

Section 6

The Talking Car

(or)

Are Your Ears Listening To What Your Stomach Wants To Tell You?

Cars can talk.

No, wait. I'm not kidding on this one. Well okay, I'll concede that automobiles don't really "talk" talk, but they do give off certain kinds of sub-auditory vibrations. You see, cars are made of metal and plastic and fibers and rubber and glass, all of which are made up of elements and molecules and whatever, and these all give off vibrations, which, when coupled with the leftover vibrations (or aura's) of the previous owner or owners, blend into a kind of signal that emanates from the center (in this case the driver's seat) of the vehicle. Therefore, you have to be sitting in the driver's seat to hear it. (I know this makes it look like I'm drifting a little too close to the yawing abyss of disbelief, but you gotta hang in there and see where I'm going with this one. I promise it will be worth it. Please note that I am smiling again.)

I encountered my first "talking car" a little over fifteen years ago while on a buying trip at a "wholesale" car dealership. The dealer was of questionable integrity (in other words, I didn't trust him as far as I could throw his whole parking lot full of cars) but I was there because he had a certain car that I was looking for; the right model, color, mileage, etc. (Yup, you're absolutely right. Not only was I breaking the "Demonopolis Rule" but I was getting emotional about a car as well. Please let me off the hook though, given that I was breaking a rule that I had not yet created.) The car looked great. I checked it over pretty well. The price was right. I wanted that car. But there was this little glitch. The first time I sat behind the wheel, I heard these words inside my head: *"Don't buy me."*

For real.

I was somewhat rattled by the clarity and urgency of the "voice". It did sound like a real voice, but of course there was nobody there. Shaking my head at my own foolishness, I got out, went into the office, and told the sleazeball guy that I'd buy the car. Then I went back to the car, got in and started it up. *"Don't buy me,"* It said. Oh my.

I turned up the radio and drove the car home.

(Insert long drum roll here.. .. ..) And the punch line is: A week later the engine blew up. Upon inspection, my mechanic found that the motor had recently been taken apart and improperly put back together. Certain things had been done to cover this up. This cost me about $2500 to remedy. (No, I didn't go back to the sleazeball dealer. Wholesale sales carry no warranty, and I knew better than to ask this clown to be a real man and reimburse me.)

"Don't buy me." It had been my intuition that had spoken so clearly.

Ever since then, I've been listening a whole lot closer to my intuition. And the better I listen, the better my record gets. As of this date, the last time I had one of those serious problems was over five years ago. Hundreds of vehicles purchased. Five years without a serious problem. *Intuition.*

Some cars really do talk. (Actually, and fortunately, its usually the sick ones that speak the loudest.) These days, even if a car checks out as great and the price is right, but I hear those little whisperings, I will not buy that car. *Even if the price is really low and its a great deal.* I will not buy that car.

Will a sick car talk to you when you're evaluating it? I believe that it very well may. What you "hear" may not be as clear as my *"Don't buy me,"* but if you begin to feel or hear things rumbling around inside you that seem to emanate from your stomach about the car you're checking out, don't let your emotions override your gut. Even if you think the car is pretty, or you're fed up and want to get it all over with, don't let that drown out the voice of the "talking car". Never ignore a *"Don't buy me."*

If the car says nothing to you then okay, so be it. But if you get that nagging feeling down there in that place where you've always "known" certain things, then pat the car on the trunk, whisper a thank you to it and wish it well and be on your way. This car doesn't want you, and you certainly do not want it.

LEITHS EXPERT SCORE CARD:

The car talks, and it welcomes you: 0 points.

The car says nothing: 0 points.

The car says "Don't buy me," or anything

even remotely like that: **-10 points.**

Leith C. MacArthur

54

Section 7

A Little Help From Our Mechanics

(or)

A Little Help from Our Friends

You've picked up this guide because you know nothing, or next to nothing (about cars) and you want some help. You need a car, you need all the help you can get. Great start.

Studying this guide and adhering to its principles will go a long way toward achieving your goal. As I mentioned earlier, the strength of this guide will be apparent in its ability to direct you *away* from a BUC, or a bad used car.

This will be accomplished with relative ease. However, I highly recommend that you have a back-up system. After all, as much as I would like to be there with you, I will not be. So, I suggest for your approval, two back-up systems: Back-Up System "A" and Back-Up System "B". Voila.

Back-Up System "A": Find a great and honest local mechanic who will agree to look over the car that you have already selected as viable (with the assistance of this guide). My personal preference leans toward small to medium sized garages that are family owned. Lots of history there. Opportunity for references, etc. If you do not know of one, ask everyone you know. Friends. Relatives. Co-workers.

DO NOT choose a repair shop that sells used cars as a side-line. They may discourage you (either unconsciously or intentionally) from purchasing the car you've worked hard to find in order that they may clear the way to sell you one of their own. There's a conflict of interest there (perish the thought) that you do not need to deal with.

DO NOT choose a repair shop that is it*self* a side-line to a large used car lot. Same reason.

DO NOT choose a new car dealer. Same conflict of motives and interests.

DO NOT choose a backyard-type mechanic who does not have a lift. You want to be sure that your mechanic can check the undercarriage for rust, oil leaks, transmission leaks, coolant leaks, leaky struts, leaky shocks, bad cv-joints or boots, rusty or leaking exhaust, etc. Many of these items are very difficult to check, if not impossible, without elevating the automobile into the air.

After doing some homework and asking around, go to the garage or mechanic that "feels" right to you. (There's that *feeling* word again). Agree on a fee for the check-over. ($40 to $60 would be fine.) Make sure that as part of the inspection he will remove all four wheels and carefully inspect the brakes. Also, verify that he will road-test the vehicle. (If he will not, find someone else.) You'll want to go with him on the test drive; if you have any questions about strange sounds or anything else, you can ask then.

[A special note regarding compression tests: A compression test consists of the removal of all the spark plugs from their respective cylinders. A gauge is then used to determine each cylinder's compression. This figure is then matched with the engine manufacturer's recommended specifications. A compression test is not usually included in the price of a standard pre-purchase inspection. If you want to ensure that the motor is in excellent condition, a compression test will help to verify this. Its not a guarantee, but it is a hedge against the worst nightmare of all; engine failure. Your mechanic should be able to determine whether your prospective vehicle should have one of these tests. The cost of a compression test varies, depending on the number of cylinders in the engine and their accessibility. $40 to $80 would be average. Here's my spin

on compression tests; they're usually not necessary unless there is an apparent or obvious problem with the engine.]

Spend the money on the pre-purchase inspection. Its worth it. However, if you cannot find a local mechanic or garage that you feel comfortable with, then let's go to:

Back-Up System "B": When you go on your initial evaluation of your prospective used car, bring a friend. An acquaintance will do, but most preferably a male. Please, I'm not being biased or sexist. Its been my experience that the mere presence of your male assistant will help dissuade your hopeful seller from *treating you like a fish.* [Remember Betty Kim?] Try to bring along a male who has that "wrench" thing going on about him. It would be real helpful if he was a true motorhead, but still helpful even if he only *looks* like a motorhead. A woman (a non-motorhead woman) buying a used car all alone is vulnerable. And remember, we do not want you to be that.

I'm giving you another weapon here in your battle against being sleazed. Please pay close attention to it. It is a tool that will help you pry the lid off the mystical aspect of the used car buying experience and get to the core of its mystical and essential truth, which is: IS IT A GREAT CAR?

Use whatever is at your disposal to unravel the mystery and uncover the truth.

LEITH'S EXPERT SCORE CARD:

Vehicle has been checked and approved by

qualified mechanic utilizing lift and test drive: **+ 15 points**

Vehicle thoroughly checked by you and your

assistant male "wrench":   **+ 5 points**

Vehicle evaluated by yourself alone, after studying

and applying this guide: 0 points

Section 8

Go Get 'Em

(or)

Go Get 'Em Twice

And now all it takes is for you to go and check it out; the car that, for the next couple of years, may be the one that's going to get you wherever you need to go whenever you need to go there. You've got you're trusty guide (me, sort of) in your pocketbook, you've got all your tools, you're properly dressed. (Seems like there's a "but" coming right here, huh?)

Well, its not really a "but", but I do have a healthy suggestion. You want to be great at this, right? You've studied this guide and done your homework and now you want to go buy yourself an excellent used car. Of course you need to be really great at the evaluation process, yes? Then how about a little practice run? Yup. A practice run. This is real easy, and believe me it will give you an extra edge of confidence when you do go out there and do the real thing.

Do you own a car now? Good. Do your practice run on your own car, in the comfort of your own driveway. Ignore the fact that you already know what's wrong with your present car. (Or maybe you really don't, and this may turn out to be a real eye-opener for you.) Go carefully over your car. Don't leave any steps out. (Except Back-up A and

Back-up B, of course.) Add up your points. Determine whether it PASSES or whether it FAILS.

If you don't have a car, ask a friend to bring theirs over and perform your evaluation on that one. (Beware. If your friend's car FAILS, they may take issue with you.) Hopefully your practice run will be done on a car that's similar to the one you're hoping to purchase, so when you do the "real thing" you'll know where everything is.

Most of all, have fun with your practice run. You cannot make a mistake here that will cost you, but you *can* gain expertise in an endeavor that could save you lots and lots of grief over the ensuing years. HAVE FUN!

Leith C. MacArthur

LEITH'S EXPERT SCORE CARD:

Practice run or no practice run: 0 Points

Section 9

Crunch Time!

(or)

Now Its Your Turn To Perform The Exam

This is how you do it. Its a sunny day. (Well, maybe not. But at least it isn't raining.) You have your tools, you're dressed for the occasion, maybe you have your male assistant along and maybe not, but you definitely have me there with you (*in the form of Leith's Expert Score Card*). Here's The Drill:

1) **Walk** around the car. Look for:

   a) Cracked or broken windows or windshield ($250.00 plus)

   b) Cracked or broken taillights or headlights ($100.00 plus for each)

   c) Does all the paint match?

   d) Any visible rust in the wheel wells?

   e) How are the tires? Insert a penny into the tread on each one. If you can see the top of Lincoln's head in any tire, that tire needs to be replaced.

2) **Stand Back** from the side of the car:

   a) Does it look level?

3) **Stand back** from the front of the car:

   a) Does it still look level, or does it sag to one side?

(If the car sags side to side or front to back, it either needs substantial suspension parts replacements, or its been in an accident.)

LEITH'S EXPERT SCORE CARD:

No broken glass or lights: 0 Points

Broken glass or broken lights: **- 5 points**

Paint does not match;   **-15 points**

Rust in wheel wells or on body: **-15 points**

Vehicle has obvious sags: **-15 Points**

4) **Look** under the car:

a) Anything hanging down? (there shouldn't be)

b) Any rust? (if you see rust anywhere, take your pointy thingy and poke the rust hard. If the tool breaks through the rust **STOP RIGHT THERE.**

DO NOT BUY THIS CAR. "Rust-through" is very bad and in most states is reason enough to fail the state inspection. Rust is expensive to repair and will *always* come back.

c) Any wet spots? Oil? Water? Green liquid? (Anti-Freeze) Raspberry liquid? (Transmission or Power Steering fluid) Any wets spots on the driveway where the car is usually parked? (If the vehicle is leaking or dripping any fluids or has wet spots yet passes your evaluation in all other aspects, then this vehicle *must* be evaluated further by a qualified mechanic. Don't purchase a leaky car without professional help. Possible big dollar repairs needed here.)

LEITH'S EXPERT SCORE CARD:

No rust: 0 Points

"Rust-through":   **-100 points**

No wet spots: 0 Points

Wet spots or obvious leaks: **-20 points**

5) **Open** the hood: (you have not started the car yet)

a) Check the oil. Is it clean? Remember how its supposed to smell? Is the level normal? (When you return the dipstick to its tube, only put it back in part of the way. You'll see why in a minute.)

b) Look for wet spots on the engine. Note: some older vehicles or higher mileage vehicles will have thick deposits of sludge all over everything in the engine compartment; what I mean by "thick" is that you could write your name in it with your finger. This would be bad. This means the engine is tired and on its last legs. (This means that you leave; Go back to the newspaper and find another prospective used car.)

Wet spots:

green or yellow   = antifreeze/coolant leak

red or raspberry   = power steering or transmission leak

dark or black   = engine oil

LEITH'S EXPERT SCORE CARD:

Engine compartment relatively clean: 0 Points

Oil level, trans. fluid level okay: 0 Points

Oil level or trans. fluid low: **-5 points**

Engine thick with grease and sludge: **-70 points**

Engine oil is sludgy , smells burned, or

feels gritty: **-70 points**

6) **Leave** the hood open and go start the car:

Listen carefully as it starts. It should fire up effortlessly and

sound normal (NOT like a Harley Davidson chopper

motorcycle or a 35 year old washing machine.)

a) Put your foot on the brake. Put the transmission

selector in Reverse. It should engage this gear smoothly

and quietly. If it bangs, there may be a problem.

b) Still with your foot on the brake, put the selector in

Drive. No bangs here either, please.

c) Put the selector in Park.

d) The vehicle is still running (hopefully). Turn the

steering wheel all the way to the left, then all the way to the

right. It should turn full spectrum without any tugs or pulls

or snags (or noises). Tugs or snags could cost you up to

$700 or $800!

e) *LEITH'S EXPERT SCORE CARD:*

Vehicle starts hard or sounds like

a hardtail Harley: **-10 points**

Steering wheel tugs or snags: **-20 points**

7) **Leave** the car running and go back to the engine:

CAUTION! *NEVER* **put your hands inside the engine compartment near the front (or to either side with front wheel drive vehicles) where the fan and the belts are spinning around. You could be seriously injured**.

a) Remove the transmission dipstick. (If this dipstick is near the spinning fan or belts, ask the owner to do it.) The dipstick should indicate that the fluid level is full (now that the vehicle is running and has been placed in and out of gear). Match the consistency and feel, the color and clarity, and the *smell* to that of the fresh fluid you tested earlier. Now that you've made your determinations as to the transmission's relative health, replace the transmission dipstick.

b) Remember I asked you to leave the oil dipstick part way out? Ask your seller to get in the car and rev up the engine a little. When he does this, watch the dipstick. If smoke comes out as he does this, the motor is getting tired. If you find yourself liking this car because it passes the tests in all other respects, this smoking dipstick (indicative of some "compression blow-by") necessitates a compression test by a qualified mechanic. (Hopefully you've pre-arranged for this.) Put the dipstick all the way back in the tube.

LEITH'S EXPERT SCORE CARD:

Transmission fluid is dark in color, smells

burned, or feels gritty: **-50 points**

Engine has "compression blow-by" (smoke

emissions from dipstick):   **-50 points**

8) **Close** the hood. Now its time to get in the drivers seat.

and check all the accessories. Turn on the A/C (if so

equipped). While the A/C is hopefully getting cold (and

if the car has power windows) run each window all the

way down and all the way up. (Repairs on some models

can run as high as $500.00 per window.) Got a sunroof?

Open it all the way and then close it all the way. Now

step outside for a moment and make sure the sunroof

has closed flush with the roof's surface. Get back in and

try the stereo tape player (did you bring a test tape or

test cd?), CD, and whatever other options the car may have. Lastly, turn on all the lights, then get out and circle the car one more time, making sure all lights, including turn signals, work. Ask the seller to step on the brake pedal for you while you watch to make sure both (or all three) brake lights work. Get back in the car. Set the emergency brake. Put the car in gear and give it just a little gas. The car should not budge.

LEITH'S EXPERT SCORE CARD:

All accessories work fine: 0 points

Emergency brake holds car just fine: 0 Points

Emergency brake does not

hold car properly: **- 5 points**

Now, you've done your exam and you've recorded your

scores. Time to go for the obligatory test drive.

Section 10

The Obligatory Test Drive

(or)

You Look Real Nice, But Can You Dance?

The main purpose of the test drive is to confirm that:

1) The car drives straight.

2) The brakes work great.

3) The engine runs fine.

4) The transmission shifts nice nice.

5) The front end is tight.

6) The car in general is tight.

If the car is a standard shift: Before you begin the test drive, set the emergency brake. Press your right foot hard on the brake pedal. Depress the clutch and put the transmission in third gear. Let the clutch out slowly until the car stalls. If you let the clutch all the way out and the car does *not* stall, this means that the clutch is slipping and must be replaced. Cost: $500 – 700 or more.

LEITH'S EXPERT SCORE CARD:

Slipping clutch: **- 25 points**

Now for the drive.

A. Go find yourself a good sized parking lot. If the car has front wheel drive, find a nice clear area and stop. Turn the wheel hard to the left until it stops. Drive around slowly in a circle. Stop. Does everything feel normal? Okay, turn the wheel hard right and repeat the process. If either circle produces a clicking, or banging, or loud squeaking sound, **score -10 points for each side that makes noise.** Any of these noises indicates faulty constant velocity ("cv") joints. Very expensive. $400 - 800.

B. Next, tighten your seat belt, put both hands firmly on the steering wheel, and accelerate forward in a straight line up to about 15 mph. Step on the brake firmly and come to a complete stop. The vehicle should stop smoothly without any chattering and without the steering wheel pulling your hands one way or the other. If it either chatters or the steering wheel wants to pull one way or the other, **score -10 points for steering wheel pull**. This means that the car has either brake or front end problems, either of which can be quite costly. Could be a little money or a lot of money. (a lot meaning; heaps, piles, and gobs.)

C. Now, drive to a secondary road. Find the bumps in the road and purposefully drive over them. (Haven't you always just wanted to do that?) Listen. Feel. Does the steering wheel still feel solid, giving you a feeling of confidence, or does it feel squirrelly and shaky when you hit those bumps? Solid and confident; no points. Shaky and squirrelly gets a deduction: **score -10 points**.

D. Now drive to a highway. Get up to your normal highway cruising speed. Listen for pings, knocks, rattles, chatters. Anything that doesn't feel or sound right? **Score - 10 points**. Get on a level, straight section of road and loosen your grip on the wheel. The car should "want" to go straight. You should feel comfortable and safe at 55 - 60 mph. The vehicle should be quiet and smooth. If you do not feel confident and comfortable, or if the car shakes or wobbles or pulls this way or that, **score -10 points.** (Or you may just choose to look at other vehicles. What I'm getting at here is that the car should feel really good to you.)

E. Okay. One thing left to do. Drive back to the parking lot you selected and stop. Sit in the car for a moment, engine running. Look at the dash board. Gauges all reading at the correct levels? No "idiot" lights on? For incorrect readings or warning lights lit, **score -10 points**. Listen. Engine still sound quiet and smooth? Good. Now get out and walk around the car one last time. Smell anything unfamiliar? You should not. If you smell anything, like burning oil, or rubber, or an asbestos kind of smell, **score - 10 points.**

Guess what? *You're done!*

I asked you to go back to the parking lot because once there you can add up your score without the seller looking over your shoulder. You should know before you return the vehicle whether it PASSED or whether if FAILED, and subsequently whether or not you want to make an offer and/or take the next step and bring the car to your mechanic. (Of course, if the seller went with you on the test drive, you'll just have to do all your tests and observations and scoring in his/her presence.)

If the vehicle PASSED, offer the seller a $50-100 deposit on your agreed price so she will know that you are serious about the car.

Now, here's my last nag: If the seller says no, you can't bring his perfect little baby of a car to a mechanic, then *go home*. (We talked about asking this question back when you first called to make an appointment to see the car, remember?) The only reason for a seller to deny you a mechanic's check-over is because he's afraid the mechanic will find out what's wrong with it. Trust me, there's something wrong. A seller should be proud to have his wonderful, well-maintained vehicle looked at by a qualified mechanic.

Okay, now you're *really* done.

Leith C. MacArthur

Section 11

48 Hours

(or)

I Just Told You I Can't Wait Five Seconds!

Please do not ignore this section simply because it is brief.

Once upon a time I knew a person to whom patience was most definitely *not* a virtue, it was just a major annoyance. I'll call her Jane. Not surprisingly, Jane was very uncomfortable with the word *patience*. And not surprisingly, Jane's life was in chaos. She had so many problems it would have required a team of dedicated therapists just to sort and label them. Jane would be struck by an idea and she would have to act on it. Now! Or she would see something that she wanted, and she had to buy it. NOW! She was obsessive and compulsive and no one was going to tell her how it might be done differently. (We all know someone like this, hmm?) One of Jane's favorite expressions, delivered like a gun blast, was *"But I can't wait five seconds!"*

Here you go: If you're anything like Jane and you are an impatient person, if you *"can't wait five seconds!"* (let me interrupt myself here.. .. .. I believe that most people, on some level, are aware of who they really are and what their most common challenges are but, if you honestly don't know the degree of your impatience, then go ask your closest friend. Whatever they say, then go with that.) .. .. ..

okay, if you can't wait five seconds then here's **Leith's "I Can't Wait Five Seconds" Rule**: Once you've found your potential used car and then successfully completed the evaluation of it by using **Leith's Expert Score Card,** and you've then followed up by taking it to your back-up mechanic, and he has approved it, and then you've put a deposit on it (*never* more than $100 and *always* by personal check) then go back to your life and - you've got it - wait.

How long, you ask?

48 hours, he answers.

And why, you ask?

Well, I once read a statistic from a national survey document regarding sales "opportunity windows". This indicates the time when a prospect (that's YOU) is most vulnerable. The survey indicated that the average American comes to the decision to purchase an automobile, and then decides to act on that decision, *WITHIN 48 HOURS OF MAKING THAT DECISION*. Wow. I don't know about you, but that kinda rocked me. 48 Hours. So, don't be average, don't be typical. Given that an automobile is supposed to be the second most expensive purchase of your life, be absolutely sure you're not acting on impulse.

Remember, **Leith's "I Can't Wait Five Seconds" Rule** is only for you dear and somewhat impatient souls who must have it now. You know who you are. And because you know who you are.. .. ..

Wait.

91

Do your homework.

Leith C. MacArthur

SUMMARY

You're mechanic passed the car: **+15 points.**

You're mechanic failed the car: **-100 points.**

Be aware. Be positive. Pay attention. Listen to your intuition. Follow these rules and the scoring system. Doing all these things will not absolutely guarantee that you will purchase the perfect vehicle, but it will put the odds in your favor, and it will put you right up there with the professional car buyers.

And finally, I will not wish you "Good Luck" because I don't believe in luck, but rather I will wish you good fun and good hunting. I'm positive that if you follow these guidelines, not only will you have increased the odds of finding an excellent used car, but you will have performed a formerly intimidating (and possibly even frightening) task with an ease and confidence you might not ever have imagined. I'm proud of you, because by reading this material to completion, you have taken an extraordinary step toward mastering the art of mastering the self.

If you have any questions for me during this process, I welcome them and will answer all. Please email me at Leith11@home.com. Now we are done.

Leith's Expert Score Card

TEST	DONE?	POINTS
saw car in sun ? (0 points)	______	______
saw car in rain (- 5 points)	______	______
you like seller ? (0 points)	______	______
you dislike seller?(- 5 points)	______	______
car "says" it likes you (0 points)	______	______
car "says" *Don't buy me.* (-10 points)	______	______
car checked by mechanic? (+15 points)	______	______
car checked w/ friend? (+ 5 points)	______	______
car checked by you alone? (0 points)	______	______
broken glass or lights? (- 5 points)	______	______

paint does not
match? (-15 points)   ______   ______

rust in wells
or body? (-15 points)   ______   ______

car sags? (-15 points)   ______   ______

no rust ?   (0 points)   ______   ______

rust-through?   (-100 points)   ______   ______

no wet spots?   (0 points)   ______   ______

wet spots/leaks? (-20 points)   ______   ______

engine clean? (0 points)   ______   ______

oil, trans fluid okay? (0 points)   ______   ______

oil, trans fluid low?(- 5 points)   ______   ______

engine grease
and sludge? (-50 points)   ______   ______

oil sludgy, burned,
gritty? (-50 points)   ______   ______

starts hard, sounds
loud? (-10 points)   ______   ______

steering wheel
tugs? (-20 points)   ______   ______

trans fluid dark, burned,
or gritty? (-50 points)   ______   ______

engine "blow-by", smokes?
(-50 points)   ______   ______

accessories fine? (0 points)   ______   ______

emergency brake
okay? (0 points)   ______   ______

emergency brake
bad? (- 5 points)   ______   ______

clutch slips? (-25 points)   ______   ______

cv joints noisy?
(-10 points each side)   ______   ______

steering wheel
pulls?(-10 points)   ______   ______

shaky ride? (-10 points)   ______   ______

pings, knocks,
chatters? (-10 points)   ______   ______

shakes, wobbles,
pulls? (-10 points)   _______   _______

engine idiot
lights on? (-10 points)   _______   _______

burning smells? (-10 points) _______   _______

mechanic PASSES
car? (+15 points)   _______   _______

mechanic FAILS
car?(-100 points)   _______   _______

TOTAL POINTS   _______   _______

0 to -40 points = **excellent**   -40 to -60 points = **marginal**

-60 to -80 points = **this is a bad used car (a BUC)**

-80 to -100 points = **a really bad used car (an RBUC)**

ABOUT THE AUTHOR

A Volvo enthusiast and professional buyer, Leith MacArthur is also a personal co-active coach, professional musician, and co-leader of the band *Planet Groove.* Currently at work on *The Finding Man,* the first novel in the upcoming William Snow Mystery Series, Leith lives with his dog and three cats in the quiet of the Rhode Island woods.

For any questions regarding Volvo's or on the process of purchasing an excellent used car, you are welcome to email Leith at Leith11@home.com.

For further information on the band *Planet Groove* and to download and listen to selections from *Planet Groove's* critically acclaimed CD's, please go to www.planetgroove.net

www.ingramcontent.com/pod-product-compliance
Lightning Source LLC
Chambersburg PA
CBHW031314060726
47590CB00003B/1206